CORNER INSTRUMENTALIST AND OTHER POEMS

by

Steven Translateur

Contents

APOLLO MISSION

Soaring out of the atmosphere in five stages,
turning another history page,
the Saturn 5 rocket hurled the capsule out into deep space,
winning the space race,
and propelling it to the Moon,
where it would soon orbit.
The intricate lunar lander,
as reliable as a good cab,
carried the astronauts to the lunar sand,
and helped set of an off world lab.
Brave men stepped foot on the surface
and were in a state of terror/bliss.
And after this spectacular extra-terrestrial roam,
the Apollo capsule flew back to Earth,
returning home!

ASTRAL ANGELS

Seraphim are impeccable responsible leaders on the Supreme
Heavenly Council.
Cherubim worship Seraphim and advise they on matters divine.
Thrones create proverbs shouted from each hill.
Dominions offer opinions that stand the test of time.

Virtues are quite ethical and administer eternal life.
Arcbeamics shine exquisitely and light the path toward exhilara-
tion.
Powers keep the peace and quell any strife.
Beamics do most of the toil so that everyone else can revel in
fun.

COFFEE

A perfect energy drink to perk you up -
joy and stamina in every cup!
Share it with comrades offering them coffee and cake.
It gives everybody a break.
It is good for everyone's sake.
Feel free to partake.
Caffeine is what makes it special
and also sensational.
There are several varieties
like cortado, latte, affogato, arabica, and espresso
that all put in a good show.
They can all make your life a breeze.
I am sure you shall agree
that it is the best beverage - as good as tea.

CORNER INSTRUMENTALIST

See the clarinetist puff out tunes
that express the ruins
of his formerly downtrodden life
filled with overwhelming strife
that forced him to the streets for remuneration.

Hear the tink tink tink of a passerby
dropping quarters in the clarinetist's hat so he shall not die
and can buy the bread
to avoid the dead
and not wither away from starvation.

Feel the thump
of the drum accompanist sound pump
as she pounds out beats
of out of the ordinary feats
in percussion.

Taste the crumpets and pies
of the bakery nearby
enjoying the concert
keeping them alert
and filling they with exhilaration.

Smell the sweet perfume
of the girl harpsichordist in the same outdoor room
as the duo come trio
who comes for tea-o
with her fiancé at the corner clarinetist expression.

DREAM HOME

Twenty rooms of every sort in a magnificent brownstone -
a well built edifice one can call their own.

A master bedroom plush in velvet
where never ending passionate nights is what you get.

A main bathroom in blue tile and with a hot tub
is where you can get a back rub.

Three other bedrooms in a patriotic red white and blue motif
where additional comrades and relatives sleep.

A stocked kitchen with every appliance
for conjuring up feasts for the alliance.

A spacious living room with tables and chairs
for throwing parties and other affairs.

A dining room for serving meals
and bargaining deals.

Another bathroom especially for guests
helps round out the nest.

An athenaeum with books galore
and leather bound tomes to adore.

A den with a stereo and large screen tv
for recreation and having tea.

A guest apartment with eight rooms
for the help or chums dancing to the same tune.

A three vehicle garage
completes the lodge.

A landscaped grounds with a waterfall,
lawn, pruned trees, and a tennis arena for playing ball.

A gorgeous wife, three offspring, two birds, and a cat
is where life should be at.

FLUTE IN THE PARK

Tooting and tweeting harmonies galore,
the flautist mesmerized the park crowd to the core.
Arpeggios of notes swirled in their heads
while completely ripping boredom to shreds.
Playing everybody's favorite tunes,
the musician performed all day until the light of the moon.
Accompanied by a brass instrument –
flute and trumpet gave melodies a new bent.
The audience applauded with delight.
The unique sounds energized the night.
Oh no here comes a heckler disrupting the sound -
screaming and shouting, barking like a hound.
The others tell him to am scramay.
He leaves, vowing to return another day.
The performers return to their wares -
and the people make donations into their hat and that is only fair.
Music provides universal pleasure
to all conscious beings by any measure.

GUM DROPS

Chewy, sweet and luscious -
over the flavor make a fuss.

Offer they as petite gifts
to comrades to make a great impression.
Stock up on they from every concession.

Tell everybody you know -
with treats it is going to snow.

Savor they in your mouth -
roll they around east, west, north, and south.

Love orange raspberry lemon
peach and banana.
These sorts have lots of fananas.

ICE CREAM LOVE

The stars sparkling were like bright sprinkles
on an ice cream sundae the day I met you!
The gleam in your eyes deemed
to me that I wanted you on my team.
The beams of joy emanating from your soul and the reams
of wisdom coming from your lips would mean
that our affection was true.
And thereafter it would seem
like chocolate, pistachio, vanilla, and butternut,
that out lives would be a cup
of the sweetest dreams.

OUR NIGHT AT THE DISCO

Hot lights flashing.
You looked dashing.
Your dress was in fashion
inciting my passion.
Energetic dancing moves
getting into the groove.
I wanted you to approve
of me.
The thump thump thump of the percussion
was stunning
because of the alluring gyration
of your body to the music.
The clang clang clang of the tambourine
made it seem
that you were an angel.
Arms flailing, hips twirling, head bobbing,
I was sobbing with glee
at the inventiveness of your steaming
actions.
And thus was born our affection
as we made the connection
 on the dance floor.
We lived merrily ever after
and was married by a rabbi and a pastor.
Five offspring later,
I can still make you purr
and have never regretted our vows at the alter!

PILLOW

Soft, fluffy, puff of joy
for resting your head and is not a toy.
What secrets it knows
from seeing love shows.
What tales it could tell
that would make you yell.
Treat it with respect always
as if it is sacred and holy.
Try two or more of them for the fun of it.
Try yoga with it to keep fit.
Match its color with your sheets.
Keep it clean and neat.
It helps you have a sound sleep
that is extremely deep.
Love it as you would love a pet
and it shall serve you well you can bet!

RAINBOW FESTIVAL

Red spangled angles splashed up and around the page.
Orange octagons serene - not in a rage.
Yellow yard sticks as mellow measures of a cage.
Green trigonometric teams working for a sage.
Blue rectangles and circles are shapes to gauge.
Indigo inversions help in reversing age.
Violet concept visions dance a rainbow stage.

SIDEWALKS

Going where you want to go,
lining up along the street,
giving something to do for your feet,
a place where you can meet
people walking their dog,
going for a jog,
hogging the pavement,
forcing you to retreat
to the lawns.
Its worse in the snow,
obstructed by sleet you know,
makes you look like a schmoe.
A fun location to take a photo:
the sidewalks of San Francisco!
Where you can greet
and often meet
celebrities with whom you can have a dialogue.

TELEVISION

An audio visual confection
with sit-coms, dramas, talk programs, and variety shows,
makes you forget your woes,
entertains and enlightens,
sometimes frightens,
occupies your time,
as good as sipping wine.
Broadcast for free in most jurisdictions,
filled with non-fiction and fiction,
shall always be around is my prediction,
a joyful, reliable comrade that is always there,
glorious, wonderful television.

THE WATCH

I remember the day that I gave you the chronograph.

It was our first anniversary and you laughed.

I poured you wine from a carafe

in the restaurant where we celebrated!

The waiter took a photograph.

The watch was adorned with jewels:

emeralds, diamonds, and rubies befitting an angel.

Since then our love has not faded

nor has it got jaded.

Our love is eternal

And the watch is a symbol of it.

* 9 7 8 8 1 8 2 5 3 7 8 7 3 *